W9-APK-693

Garfield's Almost-as-Great-as-Lasagna Guide to SCIENCE

Rebecca E. Hirsch

Garfield created by JIM DAVIS

LERNER PUBLICATIONS ◆ MINNEAPOLIS

In memory of my mother-in-law, Alice Hirsch

Copyright © 2020 Paws, Incorporated. All Rights Reserved. "GARFIELD" and the GARFIELD Characters are trademarks of Paws, Incorporated.

Visit Garfield online at https://www.garfield.com

All rights reserved. International copyright secured. No part of this book may be reproduced, stored in a retrieval system, or transmitted in any form or by any means—electronic, mechanical, photocopying, recording, or otherwise—without the prior written permission of Lerner Publishing Group, Inc., except for the inclusion of brief quotations in an acknowledged review.

Lerner Publications Company
A division of Lerner Publishing Group, Inc.
241 First Avenue North
Minneapolis, MN 55401 USA

For reading levels and more information, look up this title at www.lernerbooks.com.

Main body text set in Neo Sans Std 13/20.
Typeface provided by Monotype Typography.

Library of Congress Cataloging-in-Publication Data

Names: Hirsch, Rebecca E., author.
Title: Garfield's almost-as-great-as-lasagna guide to science / Rebecca E. Hirsch.
Other titles: Garfield's guide to science | Guide to science
Description: Minneapolis : Lerner Publications, [2020] | Series: Garfield's fat cat guide to STEM breakthroughs | Audience: Ages 7-11. | Audience: Grades 4 to 6. | Includes bibliographical references and index.
Identifiers: LCCN 2018052615 (print) | LCCN 2018055016 (ebook) | ISBN 9781541561885 (eb pdf) | ISBN 9781541546387 (lb : alk. paper) | ISBN 9781541574274 (pb : alk. paper)
Subjects: LCSH: Garfield (Fictitious character)—Juvenile literature. | Science—History—Juvenile literature.
Classification: LCC Q126.4 (ebook) | LCC Q126.4 .H57 2020 (print) | DDC 500—dc23

LC record available at https://lccn.loc.gov/2018052615

Manufactured in the United States of America
1-45567-41276-1/28/2019

Contents

Agriculture

A long time ago, our ancient ancestors moved around in search of food. They hunted wild animals. They collected seeds, fruits, and nuts found in nature.

Soon some people settled in one place and became farmers. They deliberately planted seeds for food. They raised animals as livestock. This required a deeper understanding of nature.

CORN IS MY FAVORITE CROP... AND BUTTER MAKES IT BETTER!

BUTTER

Corn got its start in Mexico long ago.

Early farmers changed wild plants and animals. They turned wild plants and animals into tame ones, making them more useful to humans. Middle Eastern farmers tamed wild sheep. Asian farmers tamed wild horses. Farmers in Mexico took a wild grass plant, nourished it, and turned it into a food we call corn.

Astronomy

Early people were close observers of the sky. They followed the stars, moon, and planets. They tracked the path of the sun. From these observations, they could tell the exact time of year. Then farmers knew when to plant and harvest.

SUMMER... MY FAVORITE TIME OF YEAR FOR NAPPING

Stonehenge

Around the world, some people used stones to mark important celestial events. About five thousand years ago, ancient people in England built Stonehenge, a circle made of enormous stones. It took them one thousand years to finish it.

Stonehenge may have been an early calendar. Its giant stones were arranged to identify the summer solstice, the first day of summer.

Ancient Greeks

Long ago, people told stories to explain natural events. When a river flooded, they said the gods were responsible.

About twenty-five hundred years ago in Greece, a man named Thales looked for natural explanations of events. Thales said rivers flooded for natural reasons, not because of the gods. He is known as the first scientist in history.

Thales of Miletus

Aristotle was another scientist in ancient Greece. He placed plants and animals in groups according to features they had in common. For example, he realized that whales are not fish. Because they have lungs and feed milk to their young, they are mammals.

DEFINITELY NOT A FISH

The Solar System

Early people thought Earth was the center of the solar system. They believed that the sun, moon, and all the planets moved around it. Polish astronomer Nicolaus Copernicus challenged this idea. In the sixteenth century, he said that the sun was the center of the solar system. Earth moved in orbit around the sun, not the other way around.

Copernicus was right—
Earth orbits the sun!

HOLD UP... I THOUGHT *I* WAS THE CENTER OF THE SOLAR SYSTEM!

Copernicus thought the planets traveled in perfect circles. In the seventeenth century, German astronomer Johannes Kepler showed that the planets took an elliptical path as they moved around the sun.

New Approaches

In the sixteenth century, Italian scientist Galileo studied the way everyday objects move. One day he noticed a swinging lamp. The lamp seemed to take the same amount of time to swing back and forth, no matter how far it was swinging. To test this idea, he set up two pendulums of equal length. He swung one with a large sweep and the other with a small sweep. The two kept time. People used this knowledge to make clocks more reliable.

Some clocks use pendulums just like the ones Galileo used in his research.

Galileo developed new ways of doing science. He used measurement and mathematics. He repeated his experiments to make sure he got the same results.

Force and Motion

English scientist Isaac Newton was born in 1642, the same year that Galileo died. He was one of history's greatest scientists. Like Galileo, Newton used mathematics to study motion. He also studied forces, which are things that cause or change motion.

I'M NOT FAT—I'M GRAVITATIONALLY CHALLENGED

Gravity is a pretty important force here on Earth!

Newton is famous for his laws of motion. His first law states that an object at rest tends to stay at rest unless a force acts upon it. So a book resting on a table will remain in place until a hand pushes on it, applying force.

Newton also studied gravity. He proved that the force holding the moon in orbit around Earth is the same force that causes an apple to fall from a tree.

Cells

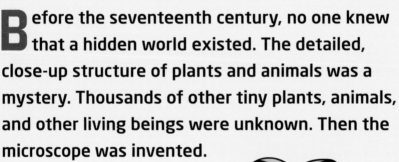

Before the seventeenth century, no one knew that a hidden world existed. The detailed, close-up structure of plants and animals was a mystery. Thousands of other tiny plants, animals, and other living beings were unknown. Then the microscope was invented.

I MAY HAVE TOO MANY CELLS

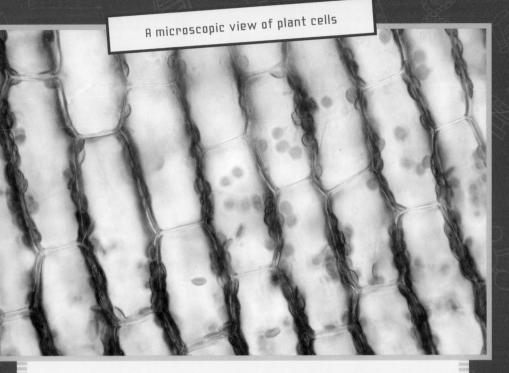

A microscopic view of plant cells

In 1665 English scientist Robert Hooke published a book showing what the world looked like through a microscope. He showed that a slice of cork was made of empty spaces surrounded by walls. Hooke called these compartments cells.

A few years later, Dutch merchant Antoni van Leeuwenhoek saw what he thought were little animals swimming under a microscope. They were one-celled organisms. Scientists eventually realized that all living things, big and small, are made of cells.

History of Life

By the early nineteenth century, scientists realized that different animals had existed in the past. Fossils made this clear. But how had so many living things come into existence? And why had some gone extinct?

In that same century, English naturalist Charles Darwin sailed on the HMS *Beagle*. He collected plants, animals, and fossils from around the world. He spent years studying his collection.

I'LL BE OKAY AS LONG AS LASAGNA NEVER GOES EXTINCT

In 1859 he proposed his theory of evolution. He said all life had descended from a common ancestor. Offspring could vary slightly from their parents. In the struggle for existence, only the best-suited living things survived.

Achievements in
IGNORANCE

At one time, people suspected that Earth was only a few thousand years old. Many people tried to figure out exactly how old it really was. In 1650 an Irish bishop famously declared that the planet had been born on October 23, 4004 BCE. In fact, Earth is much, much older. Scientists say Earth is more than 4.55 billion years old.

HEY, NOT EVERY IDEA WE HAVE IS BRILLIANT... RIGHT, ODIE?

The Atom

Ancient Greek philosopher Democritus first proposed that matter was made of tiny particles, or atoms. But atoms are too small to be seen. Was he right? The answer was a mystery.

In the nineteenth century, English scientist John Dalton experimented with chemical reactions. He showed that atoms are real. Different types of matter are made of different types of atoms. So the atoms in gold are different from the atoms in oxygen.

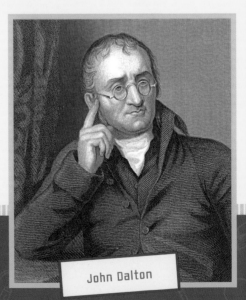

John Dalton

By the early twentieth century, scientists had discovered that atoms are made of even smaller particles called neutrons, protons, and electrons. Modern scientists think a quark is one of the smallest particles.

Relativity

In the early twentieth century, German-born scientist Albert Einstein proposed the theory of relativity. It says that space and time are woven together in something called space-time.

Einstein's theory changed how we think about time. It predicted that if an astronaut traveled in a rocket going very fast, time would slow down for the astronaut.

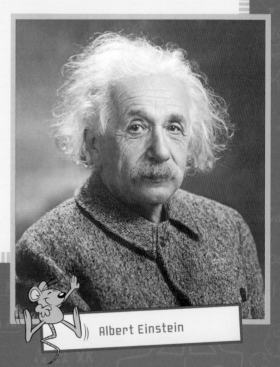

Albert Einstein

BLACK HOLES ARE COOL, BUT I PREFER DOUGHNUT HOLES... OR BETTER YET, WHOLE DOUGHNUTS!

Scientists have tested this idea. In 1971 they placed very precise clocks in airliners and flew them around the world. When the planes landed, the clocks were running a tiny bit slower than clocks on the ground.

Einstein's theory also predicted the existence of black holes. These mysterious, invisible forces exist in space. In a black hole, gravity is so strong that nothing can escape, not even light.

The Universe

Our sun is part of a cluster of stars called the Milky Way galaxy. The Milky Way is home to roughly a hundred billion stars. About a hundred years ago, people thought the Milky Way made up the whole universe.

The Milky Way is pretty incredible—but it's far from the only thing in the universe!

In the 1920s, American astronomer Edwin Hubble pointed a powerful telescope at a bright object in the sky. This object was much farther away than stars in the Milky Way. Hubble realized the object was another galaxy made of millions of stars.

Scientists believe there are billions and billions of galaxies in space. They continue to find new ones. Scientists think that only 10 percent of all the galaxies in space have been discovered.

Genes and DNA

All living things look like their birth parents. For thousands of years, no one knew why. In the twentieth century, scientists solved the mystery. They discovered that the instructions for a living being, called genes, are inside of cells. A substance known as deoxyribonucleic acid, or DNA, carries the genes. Birth parents pass DNA to their offspring.

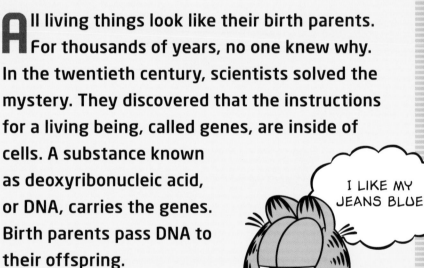

I LIKE MY JEANS BLUE

Rosalind Franklin took this X-ray of DNA in 1953.

In the 1950s, English scientist Rosalind Franklin took X-ray pictures of DNA. American James Watson and Englishman Francis Crick used her pictures to determine the structure of DNA. They discovered it looked like a twisted ladder. This shape is called a double helix.

By the twenty-first century, scientists had discovered the exact makeup of all human genes.

Breakthrough of the Future?

Advances in science could lead to new materials with remarkable properties. One possibility is a space-time cloak. It would be able to slow down time. A space-time cloak could not only make objects invisible—it could make entire events seem to disappear!

I KNOW HOW TO MAKE COOKIES DISAPPEAR

Cookies

PAWS-ON PROJECT

EXPLORE NEWTON'S FIRST LAW OF MOTION WITH THIS TRICK: Lay an index card across the top of a glass. Put a coin in the center of the card. See if you can get the coin to drop into the glass by giving the card a quick, horizontal flick with your finger. The coin drops because it tends to stay in the same place, even as you flick the card away.

Glossary

astronomer: a scientist who studies heavenly bodies such as stars and planets

celestial: relating to the sky

elliptical: having the shape of an ellipse or oval

extinct: no longer existing on Earth

gravity: the force of attraction between Earth and objects near its surface

livestock: animals kept or raised by humans to sell or use

matter: any substance that has mass and takes up space. Matter is what makes up all physical substances in the universe.

orbit: the path taken by an object circling another object

pendulum: an object, hung from a fixed point, that swings freely back and forth because of gravity

summer solstice: the time of year when the sun is farthest from the equator. The longest day of the year, the summer solstice occurs about June 21 in the Northern Hemisphere and about December 21 in the Southern Hemisphere.

Further Information

American Museum of Natural History: The Gene Scene
https://www.amnh.org/explore/ology/genetics

Chem4Kids: Atoms around Us
http://chem4kids.com/files/atom_intro.html

Farndon, John. *Stickmen's Guide to Science.* Minneapolis: Hungry Tomato, 2019.

Ignotofsky, Rachel. *Women in Science: 50 Fearless Pioneers Who Changed the World.* New York: Ten Speed, 2016.

Marsico, Katie. *Genius Physicist Albert Einstein.* Minneapolis: Lerner Publications, 2018.

National Geographic Kids: Stonehenge Facts!
https://www.natgeokids.com/uk/discover/history/general
-history/stonehenge-facts/

Index

Photo Acknowledgments

Image credits: Sana Rahim/Shutterstock.com, p. 5; Hale's Image/Getty Images, p. 7; F. G. Waller Bequest, Amsterdam/Rijksmuseum, p. 8; Aphelleon/Shutterstock.com, p. 10; Andrii Rudyk/Shutterstock.com, p. 12; Vitalij Cerepok/EyeEm/Getty Images, p. 15; Sinhyu/Getty Images, p. 17; ixpert/Shutterstock.com, p. 19; Photos.com/Getty Images, p. 20; Library of Congress LC-USZ62-60242, p. 22; Sirintra Pumsopa/Getty Images, p. 24; Science History Images/Alamy Stock Photo, p. 27.

Cover Elements: Bimbim/Shutterstock.com.

Design Elements: Bimbim/Shutterstock.com; Saint A/Shutterstock.com.